D0118802

COUNTRY PROFILES

BRAZIL

BY MARTY GITLIN

BELLWETHER MEDIA • MINNEAPOLIS, MN

Blastoff! Discovery launches a new mission: reading to learn. Filled with facts and features, each book offers you an exciting new world to explore!

This edition first published in 2018 by Bellwether Media, Inc.

No part of this publication may be reproduced in whole or in part without written permission of the publisher. For information regarding permission, write to Bellwether Media, Inc., Attention: Permissions Department, 5357 Penn Avenue South, Minneapolis, MN 55419.

Library of Congress Cataloging-in-Publication Data

Names: Gitlin, Marty, author.
Title: Brazil / by Marty Gitlin.
Description: Minneapolis, MN : Bellwether Media, Inc., 2018. | Series: Blastoff! Discovery: Country Profiles | Includes bibliographical references and index. | Audience: Grades 3-8. | Audience: Ages 7-13.
Identifiers: LCCN 2016055084 (print) | LCCN 2016056998 (ebook) | ISBN 9781626176768 (hardcover : alkaline paper) | ISBN 9781681034065 (ebook)
Subjects: LCSH: Brazil–Juvenile literature.
Classification: LCC F2508.5 .G58 2018 (print) | LCC F2508.5 (ebook) | DDC 981–dc23
LC record available at https://lccn.loc.gov/2016055084

Editor: Christina Leaf   Designer: Brittany McIntosh

Printed in the United States of America, North Mankato, MN.

TABLE OF CONTENTS

THE AMAZON RAIN FOREST

It is an early morning in June. A group of **tourists** sets off from the city of Manaus in northwestern Brazil. They soon reach the Amazon **Rain Forest** and stand in awe of their surroundings.

OTHER TOP SITES

CHRIST THE REDEEMER

IGUAÇU FALLS

OURO PRETO

SUGARLOAF MOUNTAIN

The forest is alive with noise! They hear the calls of thousands of birds and snorts of playful river dolphins. Giant turtles can be seen sunbathing on the riverbanks. The trees are loaded with fruits and nuts. Large parrots and macaws bring color to their branches. They all display the beauty of Brazil!

Brazil is in eastern South America along the Atlantic Ocean. It borders all the countries on the continent except Chile and Ecuador.

Brazil takes up about half of South America. The great diamond-shaped nation stretches across 3,287,957 square miles (8,515,770 square kilometers). The capital city, Brasília, sits just southeast of its center. São Paulo and Rio de Janeiro stand out as Brazil's largest cities. They lie on the southern border along the ocean.

GUYANA

FRENCH GUIANA

SURINAME

ATLANTIC OCEAN

AMAZON RIVER

BRAZIL

SALVADOR

BRASÍLIA

BOLIVIA

SÃO PAULO

PARAGUAY

RIO DE JANEIRO

ARGENTINA

N
W E
S

URUGUAY

7

LANDSCAPE AND CLIMATE

The Amazon River runs through northern Brazil. It is among the longest rivers in the world. Surrounding it is the vast Amazon Rain Forest. Most of this forest is in Brazil. Rocky highlands in central and southeastern Brazil cover more than half the country. The country's southwestern Pantanal region is the largest **tropical** wetland on the planet.

= RAIN FOREST   = PANTANAL

AMAZON RIVER

AMAZON OR NILE?

Some people consider the Amazon to be the longest river in the world. Others believe it is the Nile River in Africa. The debate comes from choosing the exact points where the rivers begin and end.

ITATIAIA NATIONAL PARK
RIO DE JANEIRO

BRASÍLIA
Average seasonal highs and lows

JANUARY
HIGH: 79 °F (26 °C)
LOW: 66 °F (19 °C)

APRIL
HIGH: 82 °F (28 °C)
LOW: 63 °F (17 °C)

JULY
HIGH: 82 °F (28 °C)
LOW: 57 °F (14 °C)

OCTOBER
HIGH: 88 °F (31 °C)
LOW: 66 °F (19 °C)

°F = degrees Fahrenheit
°C = degrees Celsius

Brazil's location in the southern **hemisphere** means that winter runs from May to October while summer lasts from November to April. But temperatures usually remain warm in Brazil all year. Rain falls year-round in the Amazon **Basin**. The rare snow in Brazil falls upon the southern highlands.

Brazil is rich with wildlife. The rain forest is home to a huge variety of species. Toucans pluck fruit from trees. Poison dart frogs warn predators with their colorful skin. Squirrel monkeys and black spider monkeys swing through the trees. Spotted jaguars track down prey such as peccaries and sloths.

In the Amazon River, predators such as piranhas and anacondas lurk underwater. The scream of the black howler monkey can be heard for miles across the **marshes** of the Pantanal. Marsh deer and capybaras wade in the water there.

TOUCAN

JAGUAR

SQUIRREL MONKEY

THE SEE-THROUGH FROG

The glass frog is perhaps the oddest-looking creature in the rain forest. It is lime green but has a clear belly. You can actually see through the belly into its organs!

CAPYBARA

Life Span: 7 to 10 years
Red List Status: least concern

capybara range =

LEAST CONCERN	NEAR THREATENED	VULNERABLE	ENDANGERED	CRITICALLY ENDANGERED	EXTINCT IN THE WILD	EXTINCT

PEOPLE

NATIVE TRIBES OF THE AMAZON

Around 350 tribes of native peoples live in the Amazon. Of those, 60 are totally cut off from the rest of Brazilian society.

NATIVE BRAZILIANS

Around 205 million people live in Brazil. Only four other nations in the world boast a larger population. Just over half of Brazilians have **ancestors** from Africa. Most of them also have some European **heritage**. A large number of Brazilians come from an all-European background.

Most Brazilians are Christian. About two of every three are Catholic, and a smaller number are Protestant. Some Brazilians do not practice any religion. Brazil differs from most of South America because its national language is Portuguese, not Spanish. Nearly everyone in the country speaks the official language.

FAMOUS FACE
Name: Neymar da Silva Santos Júnior
Birthday: February 5, 1992
Hometown: Mogi das Cruzes, Brazil
Famous for: A star player for the Brazilian National Soccer Team and FC Barcelona who led Brazil to its first Olympic gold medal in men's soccer

SPEAK PORTUGUESE

ENGLISH	PORTUGUESE	HOW TO SAY IT
hello	olá	OH-lah
goodbye	tchau	chow
please	por favor	POUR fah-VOR
thank you	obrigado	oh-bree-GAH-doo
yes	sim	SEEM
no	não	naow

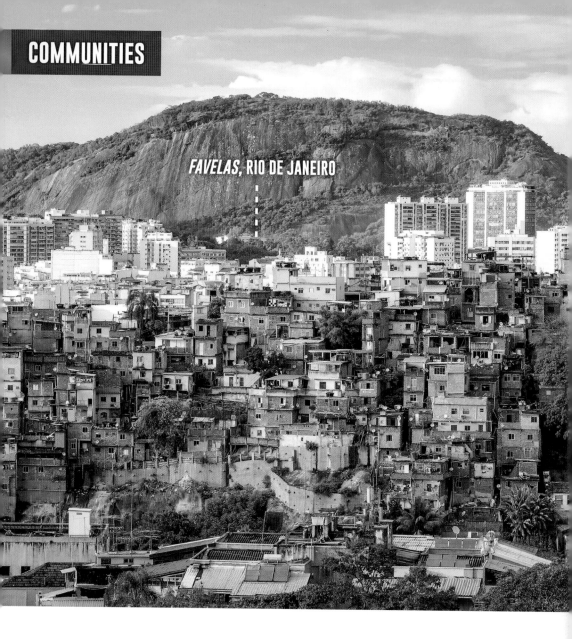

COMMUNITIES

FAVELAS, RIO DE JANEIRO

A huge majority of Brazilians live in cities. Most live on or near the Atlantic coast. In the cities, people live in houses or apartments. Those with less money make their homes in shacks called *favelas*. City travel is usually by bus or train. In the country, people often live in small stone or wooden houses. They may use cars or horses to get around.

14

Most Brazilian families have one or two children. Poorer families may have more. No matter the family size, extended families are important to Brazilians. They usually live close to one another and visit often.

CUSTOMS

Many friends in Brazil do not just shake hands when they meet. Women often greet one another with a kiss on either cheek or a hug.

Brazilians are famous for being late for social occasions. They judge when to arrive based on what kind of event it is. Some even consider it rude to show up on time for a dinner party!

The city streets serve as the center of social life for many Brazilians. The tropical climate encourages outdoor snacks and conversations on the sidewalk well into the night.

Brazilian children are not required to start school until age 6. They can leave at age 14. However, the government is working to extend that to age 17. It wants to help more Brazilian students learn to read and write so they can attend college.

Most Brazilians work in **service jobs**. The tourism industry is popular. Many work as tour guides or in hotels and restaurants. Those not in tourism often work in banks or stores. Farmers grow coffee beans, oranges, rice, corn, and sugar. Industrial workers produce cars and clothing.

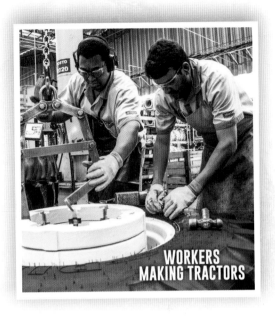

WORKERS MAKING TRACTORS

RAIN FOREST TOUR GUIDE

FUTEBOL

Futebol, or soccer, is by far the most popular sport in Brazil. Around 13 million people in the country play the game. Some of the world's greatest soccer players were born in Brazil. Other favorite sports include volleyball, basketball, and auto racing.

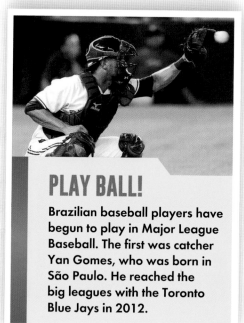

PLAY BALL!

Brazilian baseball players have begun to play in Major League Baseball. The first was catcher Yan Gomes, who was born in São Paulo. He reached the big leagues with the Toronto Blue Jays in 2012.

At night, Brazilians might head out dancing or to hear live music. Some shake their hips in a *samba*, a **native** Brazilian dance. Others enjoy *bossa nova*, a type of music developed on the beaches of Rio de Janeiro in the 1950s.

CINCO MARIAS

Cinco Marias is a popular game among Brazilian children. It is similar to jacks.

How to Play:

1. Five flat stones are placed on the ground.
2. The first player picks up one stone and throws it into the air.
3. The player tries to pick up one stone before the tossed one hits the ground. A successful player goes again, this time trying to pick up two stones. If the stone falls before the needed number of stones is picked up, the next player tries.
4. The player adds another stone each time he or she is successful. The first to get all four stones wins the game!

FOOD

GOOD MANNERS

Brazilians consider it rude to eat anything by hand. Even fruit is cut with a knife and fork!

Most Brazilians dine three times a day. One favorite meal in Brazil is *moqueca*. This fish stew has tomatoes, onions, and coconut milk, and is often ladled over rice. It can also be served with a toasted flour mixture called *farofa* that sops up the soupy liquid.

Another popular dish is a black bean stew called *feijoada*. **Cassava** roots and grilled meat called *churrasco* are also popular. All might be washed down by black coffee, which Brazilians drink throughout the day.

MOQUECA

CHURRASCO

BRIGADEIROS RECIPE

Many parties in Brazil would not be complete without chocolate truffles called *brigadeiros*.

Ingredients:
3 tablespoons unsweetened cocoa

1 tablespoon butter

1 can (14 oz) sweetened condensed milk

chocolate sprinkles

Steps:
1. With an adult, combine cocoa, butter, and condensed milk in a saucepan.

2. Cook, stirring often, for 10 minutes or until thickened.

3. Remove from heat and let cool.

4. Form the mixture into small balls.

5. Roll them in chocolate sprinkles and enjoy!

CARNAVAL

The biggest celebration in Brazil is *Carnaval* in February or March. Festivities begin five days before the first day of the Christian holiday Lent. To celebrate *Carnaval*, people dress in fancy, colorful costumes and city streets fill with parades, dancers, and live music.

Brazil celebrates its independence from Portugal on September 7. Festivities are marked by military parades throughout Brazil. Brazilians celebrate **racial** equality and **tolerance** on Black Consciousness Day. Observed on November 20, it honors a **slave** rebellion leader from the 1600s. But Brazilians do not need a holiday to celebrate the country they love!

RIDE 'EM, COWBOY!

The *Festa do Peão de Boiadeiro*, or Cowboy Festival, is held in Barretos every August. It is marked by rodeo competitions and Brazilian country music concerts.

1822
Brazil declares independence from Portugal

1565
Portuguese settlers establish Rio de Janeiro

1500
Portuguese explorer Pedro Álvares Cabral is the first European to reach Brazil

1888
Slavery is outlawed in Brazil

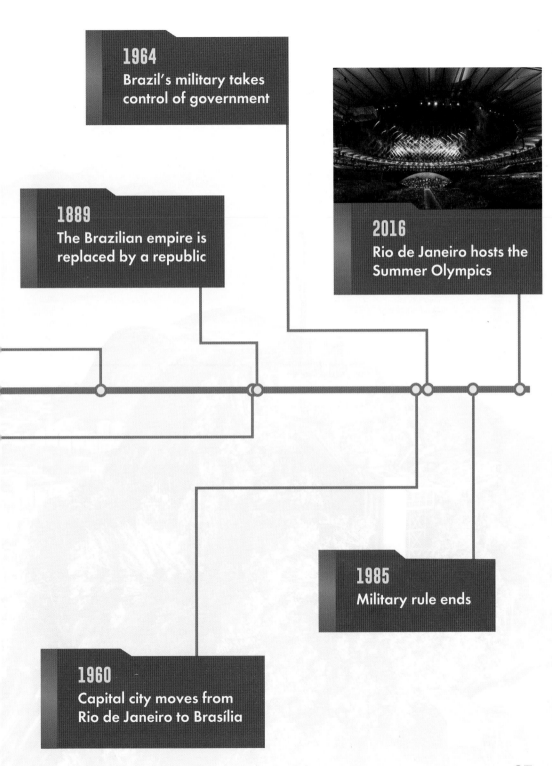

1964
Brazil's military takes control of government

1889
The Brazilian empire is replaced by a republic

2016
Rio de Janeiro hosts the Summer Olympics

1985
Military rule ends

1960
Capital city moves from Rio de Janeiro to Brasília

Official Name: Federative Republic of Brazil

Flag of Brazil: The Brazilian flag is green, blue, yellow, and white. The green represents Brazil's forests, and the yellow stands for the country's gold. Inside the diamond is a blue circle with white stars. The pattern of the stars shows how the sky looked from Rio de Janeiro when Brazil became a republic. The slogan "*Ordem E Progresso*" appears on a sharp white stripe across the globe on the flag. This means "Order and Progress."

Area: 3,287,957 square miles
(8,515,770 square kilometers)

Capital City: Brasília

Important Cities: São Paulo,
Rio de Janeiro, Salvador

Population:
205,823,665 (July 2016)

COUNTRYSIDE
14.3%

WHERE PEOPLE LIVE

CITY
85.7%

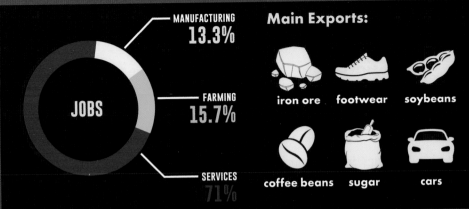

MANUFACTURING
13.3%

Main Exports:

JOBS

FARMING
15.7%

iron ore   footwear   soybeans

coffee beans   sugar   cars

SERVICES
71%

National Holiday:
Independence Day (September 7)

Main Language:
Portuguese

Form of Government:
federal presidential republic

Title for Country Leader:
president

RELIGION

CATHOLIC
65%

NONE
8%

OTHER
4.1%

OTHER CHRISTIAN
22.9%

Unit of Money:
Real; one hundred *centavos* equal one real.

GLOSSARY

ancestors—relatives who lived long ago

basin—the area drained by a river

cassava—a tropical plant with starchy, edible roots

hemisphere—a half of the earth, divided by the equator or prime meridian

heritage—the background or history of a group of people

marshes—wetlands that are filled with grasses

native—originally from the area or related to a group of people that began in the area

racial—related to people of common heritage

rain forest—a thick, green forest that receives a lot of rain

service jobs—jobs that perform tasks for people or businesses

slave—a person who works for no pay and is considered property

tolerance—fair and understanding treatment of those with different backgrounds or beliefs

tourists—people who travel to visit another place

tropical—part of the tropics; the tropics is a hot, rainy region near the equator.

TO LEARN MORE

AT THE LIBRARY

Heinrichs, Ann. *Brazil*. New York, N.Y.: Children's Press, 2014.

Munduruku, Daniel. *Amazonia: Indigenous Tales from Brazil*. Toronto, Ont.: Groundwood Books, 2013.

Ross, Stewart. *Unfolding Journeys: Amazon Adventure*. Oakland, Calif.: Lonely Planet Kids, 2016.

ON THE WEB

Learning more about Brazil is as easy as 1, 2, 3.

1. Go to www.factsurfer.com.

2. Enter "Brazil" into the search box.

3. Click the "Surf" button and you will see a list of related web sites.

With factsurfer.com, finding more information is just a click away.

INDEX